A Stroke At Midnight: Poems for the Journey from Trauma to Healing

I0107683

LaKisha Maxey

BookLeaf
Publishing

A Stroke At Midnight: Poems for the
Journey from Trauma to Healing© 2023
LaKisha Maxey

Presentation by *BookLeaf Publishing*

Web: www.bookleafpub.com

E-mail: info@bookleafpub.com

ISBN: 9798987591307

First edition 2023

DEDICATION

To my sons, Derek and Dalen. You have both lived your lives so vicariously. You have lived with intention and focus. You knew what you wanted and have worked to get it. And the journey is not over. I love to see it and I'm your biggest fan. I am so proud of both of you. You are both my motivation and the reason I fight so hard for this life. When you found out I wanted to be a published writer, you never asked me can I do this. Instead, you asked, why haven't I done it yet. I did it. Finally.

To my parents. God put two imperfect people together and made them perfect parents. You nursed me from the cradle to adulthood, then did it again after the stroke. But you never complained. If I can only be half as good as a parent as you two have been for me, then I'm doing a great job. Thank you.

ACKNOWLEDGEMENT

To my inner circle of friends who have become more like family. You know who you are. You have supported me, challenged me and made me challenge myself. This book is an abbreviated version of every day when you let me vent, cry, process, celebrate and mourn. Then get up and live life. You never let me stay down too long. You always fixed my crown. Thank you. From the bottom of my heart.

To my extended family of aunts, uncles, cousins and coworkers. Especially my "Amen Corner", The Lambrights and The Maxeys (South Carolina stand up!). What a lucky girl I am! You guys sent fruits, flowers, t-shirts, money, and of course, prayers. Three months in rehab and every single day somebody visited me, called me, sent Facebook messages, slid in my DM, texts or voicemail. They say, check on your strong friend. And you guys checked. And you are still checking on me to this day.

To the group of friends and family who didn't even know of my health concerns, you guys silently gave me strength, courage and motivation just by posting all your good and bad days. It reminded me we are all just humans trying to get through this life. And I was cheering you on from the sidelines.

Lastly to my therapists Camille and Dr Blandon. Thank you for leading me out of the dark. And to my photographer Ebony (IG: @ebonyqueenphotography) and my stylist Nikki (IG: @muni_models) and her husband DJ. Thank you for always showing up for me even when I don't show up for myself.

BIG

Dear Little Kisha,

Where do I begin?

You will get accepted to private school at a very young age because you accelerated in academics. You will be one of a few Black girls in your school and will feel like an outsider. But at home in your community, you will still feel like an outsider because you sound and act "too white". You won't feel like you fit into any box until later.

By age 15, you will end up in an abusive relationship. You'll silently suffer through that until your daddy and your brother save you.

By age 20 you will have your first baby. And by 27 your second.

You will fall in love so many times. Or what you think is love. Every relationship, you will give them your entire heart and sometimes your entire wallet.

You don't judge, you just love. So purely and effortlessly. But none of these relationships will work. You will float in and out of love, in and out of beds, in and out of jobs. By 47, you will have a stroke.

And that's when the real healing will begin in your life. You realize that you were always looking for someone to love you unconditionally because you grew up watching your parents take care of each other, and both of them took care of you and your brother.

And that's all you ever wanted. So after the stroke, you become the person you were looking for by healing your heart, mind, body and soul.

I can't tell you how the story ends, because you're a badass and the stroke didn't kill you. And you have so much more love and life to give but only to the people who pour life back into you.

I can tell you that your parents are dope, your friends are the best friends ever, and you and your kids are successful AF. You're even going to have the cutest, full-of-life little grandbaby who will call you Gigi.

Life will be incredibly hard after your stroke. But with God, you will go from trauma to healing. Stand tall. Be strong. We are already proud of you.

In 20-30 years we will ask Bigger Kisha how's life going. Until then.

I love you baby girl.

~Big Kisha

MOSES

I am Moses. I can part the Red Sea. My rod and my staff can move the waters. I have the power in my hands. I raise my face and my palms to the sky. I feel the waters raging and watch it rise above my head. I tightly grasp my rod and my staff. I am Moses. I know I can move the waters with one command. This power makes me feel strong. Makes me feel important. Makes me feel proud. I am in control. I am Moses.

I am still Moses. I can part a sea of faces. My rod and my staff can move people and avert their eyes. I have the power in my wheels. My rod and my staff are transformed into my bright pink walker. One hand clutches the rod and the other hand clutches the staff. And I simply walk. Rolling past the sea of faces that I used to command with my strut and my smile. They used to pass and wave and speak. These faces are now all anonymous. Staring with sad eyes or simply not acknowledging me at all. They move aside as I walk down the street, as if I am the bride. No more eyes scanning my face for a flirty twinkle. Now they just see my walker. My disability. My mask. I am still powerful. I can move people, but now they move away from me. This power makes me feel weak. Makes me feel invisible. Makes me feel vulnerable. I am no longer in control.

I am Moses. Watching the raging waters. Tightly gripping my rod and my staff. Arms heavy with burden and lying stiffly at my side. Face towards the sky. Watching the tide rise higher. Praying I don't drown.

JOURNEY

I woke up and hobbled past the bathroom into the kitchen. Damn, no almond milk for my cereal. I decided to go to the store.

I checked my backpack for all the essentials. Water bottle, bug spray, extra masks, hand sanitizer. I took a deep breath as I grabbed the doorknob of the front door. I pulled the door open and was greeted with the smell of nature. I exhaled and started my journey.

I used a big stick I found on the ground to move all the leaves and branches out of my way. The leaves were big and full, and hung low from the branches. I kept walking ahead despite the leaves and the bugs flying past my ears. I found that counting helped me because it made my journey easier. 1, 2, 3. I walked and walked until I heard the babble of the stream nearby. I couldn't see it but I walked towards the sound of moving water.

When I finally reached the banks of the stream, I kneeled down to drink the bottled water in my backpack. It was warm but welcoming. I stood up, checked everything was secured, and dived in. The weight of my backpack kept pushing me towards the bottom of the stream, but my strong legs and arms kept me afloat. Every stroke grew harder and harder. 1, 2, 3. Several minutes later I reached dry land and climbed out of the water. I lay there panting for a while. When I stood up, my feet slowly sank in the sand I was standing in.

I had to take big, high steps to walk in the sand. Each step grew harder and deeper. 1, 2, 3. The sun beamed directly on my head. There was nothing in sight except a few cactus trees. My smart watch said 110 degrees. I was grateful I was already wearing a mask, but my eyes burned from the high winds whipping sand across my face. Luckily, I didn't have to walk far. I could see the hill not far away.

When I reached the hill, I couldn't see the top. It was much bigger than I anticipated. I took a deep breath and started to climb. Every step grew harder and higher. 1, 2, 3. The higher I climbed, the colder I felt. I looked down and could no longer see the ground. I looked up and couldn't see the top of the hill, well, mountain. This was definitely a mountain. My smart watch said 22 degrees. I closed my eyes and took a deep breath.

Moments later I reached the top of the mountain. I stood up straight, fixed my clothes, and grabbed the door handle. I pulled the door and was greeted with the smell of bacon, egg and cheese. The Spanish music glared from the speakers and I started to dance a little. Bodega cat walked past the wheels of my walker, and I think he was dancing too. I grabbed the large container of almond milk and remembered my journey home, so I grabbed the quart size. I resisted the aisle with the chips and headed to the register. I paid and turned towards the door. "Get home safely, Mami". I smiled and waved over my shoulders.

I checked my backpack for all the essentials. Water bottle, bug spray, extra masks, hand sanitizer. I took a deep breath as I grabbed the door handle. I pulled the door open and was greeted with the smell of nature. I exhaled. I thought, it's only 3 blocks to my house but with this disability it makes it feel like a journey.

GRIEF

Denial. The first few days you lie there numb.
Almost out of body. Wondering why you're in the
hospital or bedridden. Get up. Get up. You say to
yourself. Like a small child waking mommy up for
breakfast at 6 am on a Saturday morning. Sometimes
you can't even think or cry but all you can do is count
your breaths. Be in the moment. Watch your chest
move up and down. As confirmation that you are
alive. It takes a while for your mind to realize why
you haven't gotten up.

Anger. Your first layer of reality. Questioning. Why?
Why did this happen? Why did this happen to me?
I'm not a bad person. God why me? God do you
exist? You can't because you wouldn't have let this
happen. I've been a good girl. Ate all my veggies and
paid my taxes. Then why do you hate me?

Bargaining. Ok, God or whoever is up there. Let's
make a deal. I will go to church more. I won't curse
on Sundays. I'll be nice to that annoying coworker.
Just please fix this. Make it go away. Make me better.
Now. Ok sorry but I'm impatient. Next week? A
month? Ok by summer or Easter. That's my final
offer.

Depression. Either you cry every day or not at all. Like a mother who has lost her newborn daughter or a daughter staring stoically down at her dead mother lying in a casket. The disbelief. The existentialism of this journey has ended and your soul returns to your body to offer condolences and a hug. The realization that you are in familiar surroundings and the only thing that has changed is you. The days are long but the nights are longer. People say take it day by day but some days you can only handle minute by minute (ode to Craig 🍎).

Acceptance. After the doctors tell you there's nothing more they can do. The therapists look at you with sadness. And your web browser has 102 tabs open on different ways to heal. You realize this is your life now. Then you start to heal. Mentally and physically. The mental process of healing. Where you finally look in a mirror and start accepting this new you.

Then you're reborn and life begins. Again.

THEY

They tell you you will be okay
But they don't know your name
They check the chart to confirm who you are
Before they speak

Then they say
You will be fine
But minutes ago
You didn't even know my name

They go from patient to patient
In their white coats
Doctors, Residents, Interns
I just see faces

Faces with smiles painted on
from cheek to cheek
But their eyes are not smiling
Their eyes tell the truth
They say
You're hurt, disable, damaged, dying
But inside I'm already dead

I hear a voice
He said my name
He's looking at me
Sad eyes, painted smile
Speaking words
Killing me softly

One second I am happy, healthy, vibrant
Next I wake to see the painted faces

I don't hear sentences but I hear the words
Blood clot, stroke, cat scan, therapy
They say in a sad hush tone
Do you have a mental health therapist?
I look back
I say
Do you?

How do you look at sad faces all day
And tell them what you just told me?
Or worse?
You close vibrant eyes
You paint on a sad face
Then mumble sad words to worried faces of families
I'm so sorry
They say

More words
They say
You need to move
You need to exercise
At least 60 times a day
How do you tell my body to move when I'm wishing
to die?

It could've been worst
They say
I say
Death would've been better

REPLACE

Replace my headaches with images of dancing angels. Replace the numbness in my mouth with the taste of melting cherry ice pops. Replace the stiffness in my neck with kisses from my ear to my chest. Replace the pain in my dislocated shoulder with a gentle touch of your hands as you massage the burdens away.

Replace the emptiness in my heart with songs that feel like love. Replace the pain in my back with affirmations to lift me up. Replace the tightness in my leg with the desire to run a marathon. Replace my frozen ankle with the strength of Achilles.

Replace the darkness of my depression with the happiness of laughter. Replace the despair of my hope with the excitement of my future. Replace the uncertainty of my anxiety with the calmness of the clouds. Replace the broken old me with the aspirations of future me.

BLAME

There's that dream where you always miss the bus.
Or you spend hours looking for one sock. Or she asks
you to marry her instead of breaking your heart. That
recurring dream that sometimes haunts you for years.
Or for a lifetime. You mourn a loss. If only things
went differently.

But when the loss is death, often we need to find
blame. If only I didn't go out that night. If he had put
on his seat belt. If I didn't fall asleep. If she didn't go
to the park by herself.

We blame ourselves. We blame other people. We
blame our parents. Our spouse. Our spouses' parents.
The sunlight. The darkness. The rain. The glare that
got in your eyes.

A part of me died that day. A part of me blames
myself. If only I wasn't so stressed. If only I didn't
eat fast food. If only I went to bed earlier. If only the
ambulance came faster. If only the doctors.......no.
If. If none of those events occurred then I would've
died. Then there's only one other person to blame.
God. If there's no one else to blame, can I blame
God? But is he the reason a part of me died or is he
the reason all of me lived?

INDEPENDENT

I woke up
Showered
Dressed
Ate breakfast
Drove to work
Went to the gym
Or went out for drinks with friends and coworkers
I dated
I went shopping
I cleaned my house
I lived
I laughed
I loved
Then......
Now I wake up
I drag my leg out the bed
I drag my limbs in the shower
Sometimes I use a shower chair
I lift my arm and leg into my clothes
I ask my sons for help in the kitchen
I eat breakfast with my left hand although I'm right
handed
My car service picks me up because I can't drive
I go to a doctor's appointment
Or to physical therapy
I haven't been asked on a date
I order my groceries because I get tired and
overwhelmed at the grocery store

I don't do chores often
I use to live
I try to laugh
I still feel loved
How do I ask for help when before I was
hyper-independent?
How do I say I can't do it when before I always
could?
How?
One. Day. At. A. Time.

LOVE

Don't look at this outer shell and make a decision
based on what you see
My body is weak but my love is strong
See the way my love is set up
My body can barely contain it
Love is bursting to come out of me
You thought this walker was because my legs are
weak?
No, it's to keep my feet on the ground and keep me
from flying away like a lonesome balloon
Any minute l can take flight
That's how full of love I am.

Don't let this walker distract you from what you see
in my eyes
We are all slightly bruised and battered, some more
than others
But look deep into my eyes and walk towards the
light
Bathe in the heat coming from my heart
Bask in the glory that is me

Ignore the way my arm curls like a baby bird with a
broken wing
I broke this wing trying to fly to you
I used this wing to fight off your demons
To keep you safe from harm
To shield you from the world

To cover you from head to toe so that nothing and no
one can bother you

I've always been here
Protecting you, loving you
But you ignored me because I didn't fit your
description of love
You see me and didn't see love because of my scars
But I have these scars because I am love

Real love is not rainbows and sunshine
Real love is somber days, long nights, sweaty brows
fighting battles with dark shadows and evil things
that haunt your dreams and become your reality
But you only taste cherry raindrops and smell cotton
candy because real love laid on the cross and covered
you from the hot rays of hell

You know me, you just forgot
Don't see me with your eyes
Close them
And feel me with your soul
Then you'll remember me

DIGITAL

Lonely. What a sad place to be.
But lonely and disabled is even sadder.
They say, girl, you're not disabled. You just need
time to heal. But strangers shy away cuz I'm
disabled. But it's still lonely in the middle.

So I reached out to find my digital love.
Online dating is horrible. But in-person dating is
harder when you're disabled. My walker is pretty but
I'm prettier.

So I log in, create a catchy username, add a cute
picture and l start my journey.

Three days later you found me. You said hello. I said
it back. You sent a pic. I did too. I asked for your
number. You said don't forget to call. You called me.

You were witty, intelligent, bright, funny, and
compassionate. You listened to me talk about my
trauma. You shared stories and pictures. You have a
daughter and two sons. I listened to you because you
listened to me. And you remembered everything we
talked about. You wished me a Happy Birthday. And
Happy Mother's Day.

We were in different time zones but we made
ourselves available.

You told me if I was your baby the things you would
do. Hold me. Tell me you love me. Tell me I'm
beautiful. Buy me presents. Cook for me. Treat me
special. Because I am special.

I fell in love with a person that might not exist
because he gave me everything I needed and wanted.
He filled a void when I was at my most vulnerable.

Are you a catfish? I'll never know, but what he gave
me was priceless.

SWIPE

Hug me
Love me
Kiss me softly
Make me feel safe and needed and lovely

Finding love while disabled is a task
It's even harder while we are wearing a mask

They say when you look good you feel good
That's a rule to follow
Nice skin, smelling good, even the clothes I borrowed

Despite the depression, I hold my head high
Higher than a tree, higher than a cloud, even higher
than the sky

Look left, look right
Looking for my love
Looking for the person
To fit me like a glove

Search high, search low
Search in the middle too
On land, in the clouds
Even in the ocean blue

Is it me? Am I the cause of my own loneliness?

Am I ugly? Am I fat?
Is my life just a mess?

Or is it you because you see I can't get around
You see a wheelchair, a walker, a cane
So you frown

Will my wheelchair embarrass you?
Will my walker cause shame?
Will you introduce me to friends without saying my
name?

Do you fear me because being with me will be work?
Doctor appointments, new meds, new ailments that
lurk

So I leave the real world and date online
Maybe even find someone more my kind

Someone with bumps and bruises and scars
Someone who will love me flaws and all

Swipe left, swipe right
I'm bombarded with questions
I've been idle too long, so they ended my session

What's my favorite color? What's my favorite food?
What's my favorite movie? What do I do?

But the real question is one that I have to ask you
Will you leave me when I'm sick, in pain, or feeling
blue?

Swipe left, swipe right
My inbox is empty
My suitors are low
Because I believe in honesty

I can check my camera angles
I can say I'm fine and tell lies
But then why play those games
When you can see me with your eyes

I still want a hug, I still need some love
I still need that kiss ever so softly
But being honest to myself
And being honest to you
Has been the one truth that's been very costly

Who really wants a disabled me?
So I'll make a wish and say a prayer
Until that day comes
Until you appear

HAIKU

This bitch ass wheelchair
I hate them both so damn much
This bitch ass walker

BLESSED

Yes, I have been broken, used, and abandoned. Yes, I feel too damaged to love or be loved. But it means I can't be hurt anymore. It means if you meet me now I've already seen my lowest. So now there's nowhere to go but up.

Blessed is the person that gets to experience me now. The healed version of what I once was. The healing version who continues to put the scrambled pieces of me back together.

The healing version of me that will learn how to love you the way you need. And more importantly, the version of me that is learning to love myself and can tell someone what I need in order to feel loved.

Trauma sometimes forces you into a space of solitude. It puts you in a room with four walls and a ceiling and a puzzle with a million pieces. And the finished picture is your heart, your soul, your mind, your peace, etc. When you put those million pieces together, you have you.

In solitude, I have found myself. Or rather, I am finding myself. I am now on a lifelong journey of finding and celebrating the real me. If I seem overprotective, I am. Because for the first time I'm learning how to protect myself. I am carefully putting every piece of the puzzle together. Blessed is the person that gets to experience me now. It will be an awesome journey. And I'm worth it.

HAPPINESS

The me from yesterday was fragile, worn, unsure of herself and afraid I was going to end up alone. So I looked for love in places I shouldn't be and in people I wish I never met. I treated relationships like auditions and put my everything into every scenario hoping that he can see I'm worthy or she will decide to keep me. Daily I appointed myself the fairy godmother and waved a wand to make sure every dream came true for you while I silenced myself to the point I no longer had a voice, a face or my own dream. But I had you. And I told myself that was happiness.

It took trauma for me to redefine happiness. Turns out happiness isn't in you but it's in me. It's not in me sharing myself with you but it's in me giving another person my gifts while receiving theirs. Happiness is not a one-way street that fades into darkness as I look down the road and wait for you to return home. Happiness is a roller coaster of highs and lows, that go up and down, leaves me dizzy some days and giddy on other days but all days I'm smiling because we're holding on to each other. And on the days I can't smile you hold my hand until I can.

So now I'm in the process of healing. My body, yes but also my mind. Because my body won't heal until my mind believes it can happen. So I carefully

cleanse each layer of my soul and prepare to reattach
it to my heart. Each layer requires special care. Wash
in the river of Jordan, dry on the rock of Gibraltar,
pressed with the heat of Mt Sinai, folded with
grandmother's hands, and tucked away in the family
bible.

And with each day I learn to love myself. I rebuild
the fort stronger. Toss the things that no longer serve
me. Give life to the parts I love. Fix the broken
pieces. Discard the trash.

But the warrior that emerges from the embers and ash
is a sight to behold. Like a baby giraffe. Wobbly at
first. Timid. Staying close to mother. But in a few
months, legs steady, neck long and tall, body casting
a majestic shadow on the plains of Africa. And while
my body may always show signs of my past trauma,
my mind is slowly accepting my new future. Yes, it
will be hard. But the happiness I used to seek I found
it in me. And now we will live happily ever after.

BEST

10 am
I make myself get out of bed. I didn't sleep at all. My
anxiety kept replaying the worst-case scenario in my
dreams and I'd jump out of sleep in a panic.

11:35 am
I leave the sofa and start mulling through my closet
even though I decided what I was going to wear two
days ago. But every outfit has a worst-case scenario.
Me, stepping on my long skirt and not noticing. Now
I'm standing in the middle of the crowd in my
leopard underwear.

2:15 pm
I head to the shower and stand there numb as the
tepid water ran down my body. What if I have
another stroke? In the middle of Times Square! I
imagine me, lagging behind my friends as I feel
weird and disoriented. Then falling out in the crowd.
Next to the Naked Cowboy. Then mean New Yorkers
walking by me, or worst, pulling out their phones and
recording. Some Gen Z'ers even going live as I lie on
the cold hard ground.

4:30 pm
My car service arrives and I get in the back seat. My
stomach is in knots. Not the pretty knots like

butterflies. The anxiety-laden, worst-case scenario knots. Imagine, Me, getting into a 4-car accident on the FDR. The ambulance pulls up to see my naked ass….wait I wore pants today and underwear. Ok, me, lying on the cold hard ground in the middle of the highway. At this point the taxi is getting off the exit. Ok, I didn't die, yet.

5:05 pm
I pull up to my location giving my driver a suspicious glare because we didn't get into a car accident. I stepped onto the curb, me and my walker, and roll up to my friends patiently awaiting my arrival.

9:37 pm
The car service arrives and my friends help me into the car. We pull off and jump on the FDR. As I look out into the East River, I smile to myself. I am my own worstcase scenario. I put all my energy into dreaming up the worst-case scenario, then will be devastated if it really happened. Why not manifest good energy and imagine myself enjoying life with my friends? Me, in the best-case scenario.

COOKOUT

I woke up, yawned, and stretched my arms over my head. I can feel the tightness in my arm and the pain in my shoulder, as my arm shrunk back to my side. I sighed, realizing I had dreamed I was running a marathon but it was not a reality. I sat up in bed and dragged my leg off the side. I situated myself on the bed and peeked out the window. It was a beautiful day. The sun. The breeze. The perfection of a Sunday.

I checked my phone and saw my friends' group chat was lively. Everyone chatting about our get-together later today. What they were bringing. And....Kisha you better be there.

I laid back down and talked to the heavens. Begging for freedom from my current existence. Asking for permission to die. Asking for assistance even. But not in a painful way. More like a Disney death. Where the character goes to sleep, and their playful spirit with wings darts around the room, then waves goodbye to everyone, then flies upward and enters the pearly gates. I tried to will it. I will die in 1...2...3...4...5! But the pain in my right shoulder was enough to know I was still here.

I sorted through my wardrobe to find a nice outfit and found an excuse in everything. That shirt is too tight and my affected shoulder can't get in the arm holes.

Those pants are too tight and I can't hide the brace on my leg. Reluctantly, I chose a Kisha-approved outfit and got dressed. I grabbed my walker and thought, no, I'm going to use my cane today.

The drive was serene. The driver was listening to religious music but it was in an African language. I couldn't understand the singers, but the music spoke to my heart and hugged my soul. It calmed me down. I looked out the window and saw life. Birds playing tag. Squirrels racing. Children laughing. A group of elderly people sitting in front of their building and talking loudly but everyone laughing. I missed this lightheartedness. I miss this light. I miss life. But this drive seems to be the anecdote. I could feel light shining through my darkness. Like a butterfly, my cocoon had opened and my wings stretched wide. But she waits patiently on the wind, deciding which way to fly. Watching the world made me realize not only can I run a marathon, I can fly to the sun.

The car stopped, I grabbed my cane and the oversized bags of chips (because I know they didn't think I was cooking), and I got out. I walked towards the house with the lively R&B music playing. As I started towards the house, the gate flung open and two small children were chasing a small white puppy. Teddy. As I walked through the gate, Teddy was captured and the children locked the gate behind them.

I sat quiet in a corner and my eyes scanned the room. A table full of food covered with aluminum foil. Ms.

Madden's infamous macaroni salad on ice. Two
women chatting about hair products and church. A
loud, aggressive but friendly game of spades.
Someone jumped up and slammed a card on the table.
I saw the four generations of beautiful ladies, sitting
and laughing together. An older woman, drinking and
smoking, her white hair making her skin glow as she
throws her head back with laughter. A tall slim
woman, wearing a BBQ MASTER apron, singing
and dancing as she tended to the grill. I sat and took
in the scene.

I smiled and looked to the heavens. I sighed, this was
not a dream, but my reality. I sat up in the chair and
adjusted the brace on my leg. I situated and scanned
the scene again. It was a beautiful day. The sun. The
breeze. The perfection of a Sunday.

I saw a butterfly land on a nearby fence. I think she
looked at me. And fluttered her wings. She waited
for the wind, then took flight. She told me today was
not the day to leave this earth but instead enjoy
Mother Nature. My thoughts were interrupted by
someone calling my name. Kisha, wanna play Uno?
I stood up and grabbed my cane, but decided I didn't
need it. I balanced myself and walked over to the
table. Only if y'all don't cheat, I yelled over to the
table.

Today, I choose life.

GIGI

How can your little hands hold my entire heart?

Have more? He asks pointing to the crackers.
Say please I say. Please Gigi.

He's like a warm Christmas cookie that melts in your
mouth.

I had dreams of you before you were born. What
should you call me? Where would I take you? How
would I love you?

Then the stroke.

It took my dreams and future away. It changed me. It
changed the type of Gigi I wanted to be for you.

I want to color with you
But I have to re-learn how to hold a crayon

I want to play tag
But my stiff, awkward body can't run

I want to take you to the park
But your little legs run faster than me and you may
get hurt

I want to push you on the swings
But the pain in my shoulder is too much sometimes

I want to pick you up
But some days the heaviness of my own limbs scare
me

So most days I just sit quietly and smile in your
presence

But you are my motivation

You are the reason I push forward to color, to run, to
play

Until then I just sit and stare at those little hands and
little feet. As you eat crackers and watch tv.

Go outside Gigi? No baby, no. Gigi has to lay down.
Play dinosaurs Gigi? Yes, yes I can.

Dinosaurs will keep you happy now. Until Gigi gets
better.

PHENOMENAL (ode to Maya Angelou)

Natural beauties are confused by my words
They say the things I am saying are absolutely absurd
But what I will tell you it is not a lie
Cross my heart and I won't die
It's my mysterious glare
The wave of my hair
The mole on my face
The tattoo in my crease
I'm a woman
With a disability
Disabled woman
That's me

I walk into a room with my hot pink wheels
My walker, she suits me fine, to you, she might not
appeal
Oh, she gets all the attention on an average day
People stop and stare and throw compliments her way
The shine of her metal
Her glow is just regal
The blush of her tone
I'm untouchable on her throne
I'm a woman
With a disability
Disabled woman
That's me

So God made us different. Or changed under
circumstance
Whether we walk, or roll or like a horse we prance
The next time you pass a mirror
Look yourself in the eyes
Appreciate yourself from head to toe
Because you are the prize
Give love to your reflection
And say with your chin up high
I'm a woman
With a disability
Disabled woman
That is me